TIGER IN THE KITCHEN

DONE LIKE DINNER

TIGER IN THE KITCHEN

DONE LIKE DINNER

TIGER WILLIAMS & KASEY WILSON

Douglas & McIntyre
Vancouver/Toronto

Douglas & McIntyre Ltd., 1615 Venables Street,
Vancouver, British Columbia V5L 2H1

Canadian Cataloguing in Publication Data

Wilson, Kasey
Done like dinner

Includes index.
ISBN 0-88894-561-2

1. Cookery, Canadian. 2. Cookery.
I. Williams, Tiger, 1954-   II. Title.
TX715.W455 1987   641.5971   C87-091338-7

Photography by Derik Murray
Colour separations by Cleland-Kent Western Ltd.
Design by Barbara Hodgson
Typeset by Pièce de Résistance
Printed and bound in Canada by Hemlock Printers Ltd.

All recipes indicate both imperial and metric measurements. Use one or the other—never both. Because recipes do not follow conversion tables strictly, indicated measures often are not consistent or precisely equivalent.

For the tigers in my life—Bruce, Jeff, Bob, Robert August and Casey. And of course Dave Williams.

Contents

Introduction

Teaming up with Tiger Williams was far from cookbook author Kasey Wilson's thinking a year ago. Tiger, known for his on-ice antics, was not often, if at all, thought of as a culinary aficionado. (Culinary is not a four-letter word.) (Nor is aficionado.) Few knew of his homemade pasta or how his wife Brenda works with him to prepare the meal plans a professional athlete needs. His calls to airlines to arrange special inflight meals were known only to airline staff and a few team mates.

Kasey, on the other hand, was a legend in the kitchen, a popular columnist and cookbook author with a list of credits the length of a spatula.

Then came the match.

Both were authors on the Douglas & McIntyre list, and a happenchance conversation with Tiger (plus the awareness that fans had snapped up close to 100,000 copies of *Tiger*) led to the joke that he should do a cookbook. Joke turned to serious discussion (not even publishers joke for long with Tiger!). Publisher turned to Kasey, who was already busy with *Gifts from the Kitchen* (just released). But she had plenty of enthusiasm and sports-like recipe ideas to pull it off with lots of style.

Kasey, Tiger and Brenda exchanged notes (can you see Tiger trading recipes?), comments and ambitions for the book. With this admonition from the publisher—"It will have to be the best cookbook of its kind and it will have to be as much fun as a cookbook can be"—they set to work. To the delight of sports fans and great cooks everywhere, we now have *Done like Dinner*.

And in case you're wondering—Tiger cooks the way Kasey plays hockey...

OPENING FACE-OFFS

A P P E T I Z E R S

Opening Face-Offs

Tortellini on a Stick

Tiger: *In New York this is known as Tortellini on a Schtick. I eat this in other places all the time.*
Kasey: *An impressive hors d'oeuvre. Serve with Anchovy Sauce in a bowl in the centre of a large platter surrounded by skewers of tortellini.*

20	white tortellini (egg noodle) **or** cappelletti	20
20	green tortellini (spinach) **or** cappelletti	20
4 Tbsp.	butter	50 mL
1–2	garlic cloves, minced	1–2
20	long bamboo skewers	20

1. Cook tortellini in boiling salted water until tender (about 12 to 15 minutes). Drain and rinse well under cool water.
2. Melt butter in a large skillet. Add garlic and sauté for 30 seconds. Add tortellini and toss to coat well. Remove from heat.
3. Thread tortellini onto bamboo skewers; allow 1 green and 1 white tortellini per skewer. Serve warm or at room temperature with Anchovy Sauce, p. 25.

Makes 20 appetizers.

Crustless Pizza

Tiger: *Pizza for crustless players. There is no backbone in this so we all know which players will love it.*
Kasey: *Try the variations of toppings for this speedy and unusual appetizer pizza. A big hit with the kids . . . they can make their own.*

2 cups	cheddar, Swiss or Mozzarella cheese	500 mL
	(**or** a combination of these), grated	
	oregano, basil, thyme, garlic, black pepper,	
	crushed red pepper (according to personal preference)	
1/8 lb.	salami, pepperoni **or** cooked Italian sausage	60 g
1	freshly sliced tomato	1

1. In an 11- or 12-inch (28-cm or 30-cm) nonstick skillet, spread the grated cheese evenly over the bottom. Place skillet over medium heat.
2. As cheese melts, sprinkle on seasonings and arrange meat and tomatoes evenly.
3. Fry cheese until the edges are crisp and brown. Meanwhile, fill the kitchen sink with about 1 inch (2.5 cm) of cold water.
4. When the cheese is done (edges slightly crisp but the centre not yet brown on top), remove the pan from the heat and set into the sink for 30 to 45 seconds to cool the bottom.
5. Use a fork to lift the cheese "pie" out of the skillet and transfer it to a cutting board. With a chef's knife or pizza cutter, cut into small wedges and serve immediately.

Makes 16 wedges.

Or try any of these combinations (without pepperoni and tomato):
Green onions, smoked salmon and fresh dill
Red pepper, leek and zucchini with crushed red pepper and basil
Black Forest ham, mushrooms, artichoke hearts, oregano and basil
Onions, anchovies, black olives, basil and oregano
Red onion, garlic, crabmeat, artichoke hearts, green olives, capers, pine
    nuts

Fried Chicken or Turkey Nuggets

Tiger: *Even the Flames couldn't stand the heat in the south. Bite-sized for the once-bitten, twice shy. There are no chickens on my team—they are all in my cookbook.*

Kasey: *These tasty turkey or chicken tidbits will disappear in minutes.*

2 lbs.	chicken or turkey cutlets	1 kg
1/3 cup	flour	75 mL
1/2 tsp.	salt	2 mL
2 tsp.	dried parsley flakes	10 mL
1 tsp.	oregano	5 mL
	freshly ground pepper	
	vegetable oil	

1. Slice cutlets into 2-inch (5-cm) pieces.
2. Heat 1/4–1/2 inch (5 mm–1 cm) oil in large heavy skillet. Mix flour, salt, parsley, oregano and pepper together in paper bag. Shake meat pieces in bag until thoroughly coated. Place in hot oil just until lightly browned and tender. Drain on paper towels and serve immediately with sauces.

Serves 8.

Sweet and Sour Sauce

1/3 cup	pineapple juice	75 mL
1 Tbsp.	cornstarch	15 mL
1/2 cup	maple syrup	125 mL
1/4 cup	vinegar	50 mL
2 Tbsp.	soy sauce	25 mL
2 Tbsp.	ketchup	25 mL
1 large	garlic clove, minced	1 large

In a small saucepan, combine well juice and cornstarch. Add remaining ingredients and bring mixture to a boil. Reduce heat to simmer and stir until thickened.

Makes about 1 cup (250 mL).

Apple Mustard Sauce

Mix equal parts of apple jelly and Dijon mustard **or** prepared mustard over medium heat and stir until combined.

Buffalo Left and Right Chicken Wings

Tiger: *In hockey most chickens are turkeys, and I have little respect for either except when they have met their maker—a deep-fryer.*

Blue Cheese Dip

2 Tbsp.	finely chopped onion	25 mL
1	garlic clove, minced	1
1/4 cup	chopped fresh parsley	50 mL
1 cup	mayonnaise	250 mL
1/2 cup	sour cream	125 mL
1/4 cup	crumbled blue cheese	50 mL
1 Tbsp.	lemon juice	15 mL
1 Tbsp.	white vinegar	15 mL
	salt and freshly ground pepper to taste	
	pinch of cayenne pepper	

In a medium bowl, combine all ingredients, stirring well. Chill for at least 30 minutes.

Wings

4 lbs.	chicken wings (24–28)	2 kg
	vegetable oil for deep frying	
1/2 cup	unsalted butter	125 mL
1/4 cup	Tabasco sauce	50 mL
	celery sticks	
	Blue Cheese Dip	

1. Cut wings into 3 pieces at the joints. Discard the tips or reserve for stock. Pat chicken dry.
2. In a deep-fryer or a deep, heavy skillet, heat oil to 385°F (200°C). Fry the chicken in batches until crisp and golden brown (about 10 minutes). Drain on paper towels.
3. In a large skillet, melt the butter over low heat and add the Tabasco.
4. Add the chicken to the hot butter sauce and toss to thoroughly coat each piece.
5. Serve with celery sticks and Blue Cheese Dip. Serves 4–6.

Tortellini on a Stick (p. 13), Get-Stuffed Mushroom Helmets (p. 27) and Vegetable Hat Trick (p. 24-25) with, from the back, Blue Cheese Dip (p. 16), Shrimp Dip (p. 24) and Anchovy Sauce (p. 25)

Lox, Stock and Bagels

Tiger: *What can you say about dried fish and hard bread, except that this is what the animals in New York eat with the beer they pour on the players. The ingredients are appropriately simple.*
Kasey: *If you are unable to purchase mini-bagels, use regular bagels, cut in half horizontally and then cut in quarters. You may want to pack the salmon mixture into a crock and serve surrounded by bagels.*

8-oz. pkg.	cream cheese, at room temperature	250-g pkg.
1/4 lb.	smoked salmon, in small slices	125 g
1/4 cup	sour cream	50 mL
2 tsp.	fresh dill	10 mL
2 tsp.	capers **(optional)**	10 mL
1/4 cup	chopped green onion	50 mL
12	mini-bagels, cut in half horizontally	12
	fresh dill for garnish	

1. In the bowl of a food processor, using metal blade, blend together cream cheese, smoked salmon, sour cream and dill. Process until smooth, scraping the bowl often.
2. Fold capers and green onion into salmon mixture and spread on mini-bagels. Garnish with fresh dill.

Makes 2 dozen pieces.

Montreal Omelette (p. 44) with French rolls and a Bloody Mary

Thick Skins

Tiger: *Dedicated to those among the elite in the pen and pencil crowd, especially the girl in Toronto.*
Kasey: *This recipe proves potato skins' outsides are as good as the insides— maybe better.*

4	potatoes, unpeeled	4
1/4 cup	butter, melted	50 mL
	salt and pepper	

1. To make baked potato wedges: Scrub potatoes, dry and pierce with a fork. Bake at 400°F (200°C) until tender (about 45 minutes). Cool slightly and cut into wedge-shaped quarters. Remove pulp, leaving about 1/4–1/2 inch (5 mm–1 cm) shell.
2. Brush with melted butter, sprinkle with salt and pepper, and bake until crispy (about 10 minutes).

Makes 16 wedges.

Bacon Cheddar Potato Skins

8 slices	cooked bacon, crumbled	8 slices
1/2 cup	chopped green onions	125 mL
1 cup	grated cheddar cheese	250 mL
1 tsp.	paprika	5 mL
1 tsp.	salt	5 mL
1/2 tsp.	freshly ground pepper	2 mL
16	baked potato wedges	16

1. Preheat oven to 425°F (220°C).
2. Combine bacon, onions, cheese, paprika, salt and pepper. Sprinkle on top of each potato wedge.
3. Bake until cheese melts (about 8 to 10 minutes). Serve immediately.

Makes 16 wedges.

Chili Potato Skins

4	canned green chilies, rinsed, seeded and chopped	4
1 cup	grated Monterey Jack cheese	250 mL
1/2 cup	chopped green onions	125 mL
16	baked potato wedges	16

1. Preheat oven to 425°F (220°C).
2. Combine chilies, cheese and green onions. Sprinkle on top of each potato wedge.
3. Bake until cheese melts (about 8 to 10 minutes). Serve immediately.

Makes 16 wedges.

Cheddar Beer Spread

Tiger: *Some people like hot tubs, some people like Cheddar Beer Spread. Remove cap before spreading beer. As Canadian as apple pie.*
Kasey: *Cheddar Beer Spread keeps two weeks in the refrigerator.*

2-1/2 cups	grated old cheddar cheese	625 mL
2	garlic cloves, minced	2
1/2 tsp.	dry mustard	2 mL
1 Tbsp.	Worcestershire sauce	15 mL
2 drops	Tabasco sauce	2 drops
	salt	
1/2 cup	warm beer	125 mL

1. In a mixing bowl, combine cheese, garlic, mustard, Worcestershire sauce, Tabasco sauce and salt. Gradually beat in beer. Adjust seasonings to taste.
2. Pack spread into crocks, small soufflé dishes or custard cups, filling to the brim. Refrigerate overnight so flavours can blend. Serve with crackers or cocktail bread.

Makes 2 cups (500 mL).

Swedish Meatballs

Tiger: *I always said those guys are different. Now I've done it up in ground meat so you can see what I mean.*
Kasey: *For an appetizer serve in a chafing dish with picks. For a main course serve with Swedish Cream Sauce along with Gordie Howe's Legendary Rice and a salad.*

1/2 cup	fine dry breadcrumbs	125 mL
1/2 lb.	ground beef	225 g
1/2 lb.	ground veal	225 g
1/2 lb.	ground pork	225 g
1 small	onion, finely chopped	1 small
1 cup	milk	250 mL
2	eggs, beaten	2
1-1/2 tsp.	salt	7 mL
1/2 tsp.	pepper	2 mL
1 tsp.	Worcestershire sauce	5 mL
1/2 tsp.	nutmeg	2 mL
2 Tbsp.	butter	25 mL
2 Tbsp.	oil	25 mL

1. In a large bowl, combine all ingredients and mix lightly but thoroughly with your hands.
2. Shape into 1-inch (2.5-cm) balls, place on a baking sheet and refrigerate for 1 hour.
3. Melt butter and oil in a heavy skillet over high heat. Add meatballs, about 10 at a time, and reduce heat to medium. Shake pan constantly, rolling meatballs for approximately 8 minutes until no pink is visible when balls are cut in half. Remove meatballs to a baking dish and keep warm in a 200°F (100°C) oven. Repeat for remaining meatballs, adding more butter and oil to skillet as needed. Reserve pan drippings to make Swedish Cream Sauce.

Makes 50–60 meatballs.

Swedish Cream Sauce

2 Tbsp.	flour	25 mL
	pan drippings	
1 cup	consommé **or** beer	250 mL
1-1/2 cups	light cream	375 mL
	salt and pepper to taste	
1/2 tsp.	caraway seeds **(optional)**	2 mL

Stir flour into pan drippings and slowly blend in consommé **or** beer. Add cream and cook until thickened but still slightly thin. Season to taste with salt and pepper, and add caraway seeds if desired.

Vegetable Hat Trick

Tiger: *I always treat the opposition with this when they cross me. My only complaint is that I don't get enough. Three times lucky. And give me a break! Shrimp Dip is solely for tiny peewee hockey players.*
Kasey: *Beautiful colours and flavours. Shrimp Dip is always in danger of disappearing before it reaches the guests. Equally delicious with fresh crab meat.*

Fill a basket or serving tray with an assortment of your favourite vegetables and serve with Shrimp Dip (page 24), Anchovy Sauce (page 25) and Blue Cheese Dip (page 16).

asparagus	jicama spears
broccoli	fresh mushrooms
carrot sticks	strips of green/red/orange/yellow
cauliflowerets	pepper
celerey sticks	red or white radishes
cucumbers	snow peas
green onions	cherry tomatoes
zucchini	

Shrimp Dip

1 cup	commercial salad dressing	250 mL
1 cup	mayonnaise	250 mL
1/2 lb.	cream cheese, at room temperature	250 g
1/2 cup	diced celery	125 mL
1/2 cup	chopped green onions	125 mL
1/4 cup	horseradish	50 mL
	juice of 1 lemon	
	dash of Worcestershire sauce	
1/2 lb.	fresh cooked shrimp, cut in thirds	250 g

Combine salad dressing, mayonnaise, cream cheese and blend until smooth. Stir in celery, onions, horseradish, lemon juice, Worcestershire sauce and shrimps. Refrigerate overnight so flavours can blend.

Makes about 4 cups (1 L).

Anchovy Sauce

1 cup	mayonnaise	250 mL
1 cup	sour cream	250 mL
2	garlic cloves, minced	2
4	anchovy fillets, finely minced	4
1 Tbsp.	vodka **(optional)**	15 mL
2 Tbsp.	lemon juice	25 mL
2 Tbsp.	chopped fresh parsley	25 mL
2 tsp.	minced chives	10 mL

Blend all ingredients and chill well.

Makes 2 cups (500 mL).

Mussel-Stuffed Mushrooms

Tiger: *Gary Nylund used to get stuffed on these before he went east. When the season's over, he can't wait to return to the west.*
Kasey: *Mussels replace escargots in this heady garlic butter combination.*

32	mussels, in shells	32
1 cup	unsalted butter, softened	250 mL
2 tsp.	garlic, minced	10 mL
2 Tbsp.	finely chopped green onion	25 mL
2 Tbsp.	chopped parsley	25 mL
1/2 tsp.	salt	2 mL
1/4 tsp.	pepper	1 mL
1/2 cup	bread crumbs	125 mL
32 large	fresh mushroom caps	32 large
1	lemon, cut in eighths	1

1. Place mussels in a large saucepan and add 1/2 inch (1 cm) water, dry white wine or beer. Cover and steam over medium-high heat only until the mussel shells open wide. Discard any that do not open. Drain and shuck the mussels.
2. In a small bowl blend 3/4 cup (175 mL) butter with garlic, onion, parsley, salt and pepper. Melt remaining butter in a large skillet. Add bread crumbs and toss in butter to coat. Remove from heat.
3. Twist stems carefully from caps. Arrange caps bottom-up on a buttered baking sheet. Place 1 mussel in each cap. Top with 1 tsp. (5 mL) each of the garlic butter and bread crumbs. Cover and refrigerate until final baking.
4. Bake at 450°F (230°C) for 10 minutes or until crumbs are just browned.

Serves 6–8.

Get-Stuffed Mushroom Helmets

Tiger: *Sure tastier than **our** helmets.*
Kasey: *Use fresh, plump white or brown cultivated mushrooms for these crab-stuffed appetizers—a favourite of Tiger's.*

30	large fresh mushrooms	30
1/4 cup	cream cheese	125 g
2 Tbsp.	mayonnaise	25 mL
1 Tbsp.	Dijon mustard	15 mL
6 oz.	fresh crabmeat	200 g
2 Tbsp.	finely chopped red **or** green pepper	25 mL
1 Tbsp.	finely chopped green onion	15 mL
2 tsp.	fresh lemon juice	10 mL
1/2 cup	grated Swiss Gruyere cheese	125 mL
	freshly ground pepper and salt to taste	
10-oz. can	mandarin orange segments	284-mL can

1. Preheat oven to 375°F (190°C).
2. Wipe mushrooms with a damp paper towel. Twist stems carefully from caps.
3. Combine cream cheese, mayonnaise and mustard and blend well. Add crabmeat, red **or** green pepper, green onion, lemon juice, cheese, pepper and salt and stir well.
4. Stuff crabmeat mixture into mushroom caps and place a mandarin orange segment on top of each mushroom.
5. Bake for 10 to 15 minutes or until hot and bubbly.

Makes 30.

Red Russian Nut Puffs

Tiger: *Harold Ballard's fantasy of what he'd like to serve at Maple Leaf Gardens, but this would never be served there because Russian-bashing is popular when Harold's in attendance.*

Kasey: *Serve these savoury puffs straight from the oven. If you prefer puffs with some extra bite, use Asiago or Old Gouda cheese.*

1 cup	water	250 mL
1/2 cup	butter	125 mL
1 cup	all purpose flour	250 mL
1/4 tsp.	salt	1 mL
4 large	eggs, at room temperature	4 large
2/3 cup	grated Swiss Gruyere, Asiago **or** Old Gouda cheese	150 mL
1/2 cup	finely chopped Macadamia nuts	125 mL

1. Preheat oven to 400°F (200°C).
2. Heat the water and butter in a 2-quart (2-L) saucepan over moderate heat until water boils and butter melts. Add flour and salt all at once. Remove from heat and stir vigorously until mixture leaves side of pan and begins to form a ball.
3. Add eggs one at a time, beating well after each addition. Continue to beat until mixture is smooth and glossy. Stir in cheese and Macadamias.
4. Shape into 1-inch (2.5-cm) balls and place about 1 inch (2.5 cm) apart on a large greased cookie sheet. Bake 10 minutes. Reduce heat to 350°F (180°C) and bake until puffed and golden brown (about 25 to 30 minutes). Serve at once.

Makes about 2-1/2 dozen cocktail-size puffs.

Note: *Russian Nut Puffs may be frozen. To reheat, arrange frozen puffs on cookie sheet and place in a 400°F (200°C) oven just until thawed and surface is crisp. Serve at once.*

FIRST PERIOD

SALADS AND SOUPS
First Period

Offensive Salad

Tiger: *No wonder Edmonton is so good—they all eat this. This is my best ally when I'm ripping off someone's helmet.*
Kasey: *This exotic salad is from the Middle East. Serve with Stickhandler's Shish Kebab and Gordie Howe's Legendary Rice.*

3	tomatoes, skinned, seeded and chopped (juice reserved)	3
1 large	red **or** Spanish onion, chopped	1 large

Dressing

	reserved juice from tomatoes	
2 Tbsp.	olive oil	25 mL
1 Tbsp.	vinegar	15 mL
1 large	garlic clove, minced	1 large
1/2 tsp.	ground cumin seed	2 mL
1/2 tsp.	sweet paprika	2 mL
	salt and pepper to taste	
1 Tbsp.	finely chopped fresh parsley	15 mL

Mix thoroughly and combine with tomatoes and onions.

Serves 4–6.

Mexican Chicken Salad

Tiger: *For all those who didn't quite make it, this stuff will really make the ice melt. A favourite for those chili lovers.*
Kasey: *Canned chilies are interchangeable in recipes calling for fresh.*

1 large head	iceberg lettuce	1 large head
4	flour tortillas	4
	oil for frying	
1/4 cup	minced green onions	50 mL
16	black olives, halved	16
16	cherry tomatoes, halved	16
4 cups	shredded cooked chicken	1 L
1-1/2 cups	julienned jicama (see Note)	375 mL
1 large	avocado, peeled and sliced	1 large
1/3 cup	shelled sunflower seeds	75 mL
	Green Chili Dressing	

1. Core, rinse and thoroughly drain lettuce. Shred and place in plastic bag in refrigerator to crisp.
2. In wide skillet over medium heat, fry tortillas, one at a time, in about 1/4 inch (5 mm) oil until just crisp and light brown. Drain on paper towels. Place each tortilla on dinner plate.
3. Divide lettuce among 4 plates, spreading almost to edges of tortillas. Sprinkle lettuce evenly with green onions and arrange on top olives, tomatoes, chicken, jicama and avocado. Sprinkle with sunflower seeds. Serve with Green Chili Dressing.

Note: *Jicama (pronounced "hee-kah-mah") is a Mexican vegetable that looks like a brown turnip and tastes like a cross between an apple and a water chestnut.*

Serves 4.

Green Chili Dressing

1/4 cup	sour cream	50 mL
1/4 cup	diced green chilies	50 mL
1/4 cup	lime juice	50 mL
2 Tbsp.	oil	25 mL
1/4 tsp.	Tiger's Seasoned Salt (page 51)	1 mL
2 Tbsp.	finely chopped green onions	25 mL
	dash of Tabasco sauce	

In medium bowl, combine all ingredients. Mix well and refrigerate until needed.

Semi-Final Spinach Salad

Tiger: *Popeye was right, kids. It will get you this far, and then you are on your own. Perfect for a group of hockey fans.*
Kasey: *Team up with Bantam Turkey Chili and French bread.*

1-1/2 lbs.	fresh spinach, washed and trimmed	750 g
1/2 lb.	fresh mushrooms, sliced	250 g
1/4 lb.	bacon, cooked and crumbled	125 g
1-1/2 cups	bean sprouts	375 mL
2 medium	red onions, thinly sliced	2 medium
2 tsp.	Dijon mustard	10 mL
2 Tbsp.	finely chopped green onions	25 mL
1 cup	olive oil	250 mL
1/4 cup	tarragon wine vinegar	50 mL
1 Tbsp.	sugar	15 mL
	salt and freshly ground pepper to taste	

1. Tear spinach into bite-sized pieces and place in very large mixing bowl. Add mushrooms, bacon, bean sprouts and onions and toss thoroughly.
2. In a container with a tight-fitting lid, combine mustard, green onions, oil, vinegar and sugar. Shake well and add salt and pepper to taste. Shake again and pour dressing over salad. Serve immediately.

Serves 10.

Defensive Salad

Tiger: *I call this Defensive Salad in honour of Philadelphia and Montreal who consistently play the style that wins.*
Kasey: *This colourful, crisp salad is delicious with Swift Current Casserole.*

1/2 cup	mayonnaise	125 mL
1/4 cup	sour cream	50 mL
3 Tbsp.	sugar	45 mL
2 Tbsp.	white wine vinegar	25 mL
1/3 cup	olive oil	75 mL
1	garlic clove, minced	1
2 tsp.	Dijon mustard	10 mL
1/8 tsp.	celery salt	0.5 mL
1/8 tsp.	freshly ground black pepper	0.5 mL
1 Tbsp.	lemon juice	15 mL
1/2 cup	light cream	125 mL
1/2 tsp.	salt	2 mL
1 small head	green cabbage, finely shredded	1 small head
1/2 head	red cabbage, finely shredded	1/2 head
2	carrots, coarsely grated	2
1	green pepper, finely chopped	1
2	green onions, finely sliced	2

1. Blend together mayonnaise, sour cream, sugar, vinegar and olive oil. Add garlic, mustard, celery salt, pepper, lemon juice, cream and salt. Stir until smooth.
2. In a separate bowl, combine cabbages, carrots, green pepper and green onions.
3. Pour dressing over vegetables and toss until well coated.

Serves 8–10.

Referee's Pasta (p. 61) with smoked salmon, Parmesan cheese, Semi-Final Spinach Salad (p. 33) and white wine

Boston Bruins Clam Chowder

Tiger: *This is a hearty soup for my kind of team. Dedicated to Terry O'Reilly.*
Kasey: *Boston's always claimed to have the best chowder—no flour and no tomatoes—and we agree.*

3-1/2 lbs.	fresh clams, in shells	1.5 kg
1 cup	water	250 mL
1 cup	white wine	250 mL
1/4 lb.	bacon	125 g
2 medium	onions, chopped	2 medium
3 medium	potatoes, peeled and diced	3 medium
1-1/2 cups	milk, scalded	375 mL
1 cup	whipping cream	250 mL
	freshly ground black pepper	
	pinch of dried thyme	
	salt to taste	
2 Tbsp.	butter	25 mL

1. Place clams in water to cover for 30 minutes. Scrub with a stiff brush and discard any clams with cracked shells. Steam in 1 cup (250 mL) water and
1 cup (250 mL) wine over medium-high heat until shells open (about 8 minutes). Discard clams that do not open. Remove clams and set aside.
2. Strain broth through cheesecloth to remove sand and bits of shells. Set broth aside. Dice clams.
3. In a medium-sized saucepan, cook bacon until crisp. Remove bacon with a slotted spoon and reserve. Add onions and potatoes and sauté until onions are tender. Add scalded milk, cream, clam broth, chopped clams and bacon. Add pepper and thyme. Heat slowly but do not let boil. Season with salt.
4. Ladle chowder into bowls and top each serving with a pat of butter.

Serves 4.

Stickhandler's Shish Kebab (p. 80-81), Offensive Salad (p. 31), Gordie Howe's Legendary Rice (p. 55) and beer

Baked Chicken Soup

Kasey: *Creamy and rich, this simple soup hails from Wales (Castle Hotel, Conway)...*
Tiger: *... and is fit for an L.A. King.*

1/3 cup	butter	75 mL
1/3 cup	sliced carrots	75 mL
1/3 cup	chopped celery	75 mL
1/2 cup	chopped onion	125 mL
2 slices	bacon, diced	2 slices
1-1/3 cups	diced cooked chicken	300 mL
1 tsp.	*fines herbes*	5 mL
1/3 cup	flour	75 mL
2 cups	chicken stock	500 mL
	whipping cream	
	Parmesan cheese	

1. In a large skillet over medium-high heat, melt butter. Sauté carrots, celery and onion until tender. Add bacon, chicken, and *fines herbes*. Stir in flour until smooth. Reduce heat to medium-low and gradually add chicken stock. Blend well, stirring constantly, and bring to a boil. If soup is too thick, thin with additional chicken stock.
2. Pour soup into bowls and swirl whipping cream on top. Sprinkle with Parmesan cheese and broil until cheese browns.

Serves 2.

Cheesy Beer Chowder

Tiger: *This is what I eat when I'm in the penalty box, so this recipe is dedicated to the officials who are always sending me there.*
Kasey: *Great on a cold winter day!*

1/4 cup	butter	50 mL
1/4 cup	flour	50 mL
1 tsp.	salt	5 mL
1/2 tsp.	dry mustard	2 mL
2 cups	milk, scalded	500 mL
1 tsp.	Worcestershire sauce	5 mL
2 cups	grated old cheddar cheese	500 mL
12-oz. can	beer	341-mL can
	salt and pepper to taste	
	Cheese Croutons for garnish	

In a heavy saucepan over medium heat, melt butter. Blend in flour, salt and mustard. Add Worcestershire sauce and scalded milk and stir until smooth and thickened. Add cheese. Stir until cheese is melted. Add beer and season with salt and pepper. Heat soup through but do not boil. Serve with Cheese Croutons.

Serves 4–6.

Cheese Croutons

butter and olive oil
French bread, cut in 1/2-inch (1-cm) cubes or slices
grated Parmesan cheese

Melt butter with oil in frying pan. Sauté bread until evenly browned. Sprinkle with Parmesan cheese. Add to hot soup or serve croutons separately in a bowl.

OFFSIDES

Offsides

Kings Pocket Pita with Crab

Tiger: *As Doctor Buss knows, all pitas have pockets but not all pockets have pitas. Marcel wishes he was still in L.A. to enjoy this.*
Kasey: *A pocket that forms while this Middle Eastern bread is baking makes it ideal for a large variety of hearty sandwich fillings.*

1/2 lb.	fresh crabmeat	250 g
1/2 lb.	medium cheddar cheese, grated	250 g
2/3 cup	mayonnaise	175 mL
1 Tbsp.	fresh dill	15 mL
1 cup	coarsely chopped black olives	250 mL
1	avocado, thinly sliced	1
4	pita bread, halved	4

1. Preheat oven to 300°F (150°C).
2. Combine crabmeat, cheese, mayonnaise, dill, black olives and avocado and mix well. Stuff halved pita bread with filling, wrap in foil and bake until piping hot (about 20 minutes).

Serves 4–6.

Montreal Omelette

Tiger: *I thought it was the Montreal Alouettes, but I got it a little scrambled.*
At home, I use sauerkraut or smoked meat in it.
Kasey: *Omelettes are the most versatile use of the egg. This and the following*
omelettes may be eaten as a main dish for brunch or lunch. They are ideal
for a last-minute dinner.

2 Tbsp.	butter	25 mL
1/4 cup	chopped onion	50 mL
1/4 cup	chopped green pepper	50 mL
1 cup	sauerkraut, drained and rinsed	250 mL
1/4 lb.	shaved corned beef **or** pastrami	125 g
8	eggs	8
3 Tbsp.	water	45 mL
1 tsp.	salt	5 mL
1/4 tsp.	pepper	1 mL
4 Tbsp.	butter	60 mL
1/2 cup	grated Swiss cheese	125 mL
4	French bread rolls	4
1/4 cup	Thousand Island dressing	60 mL

1. In a skillet, melt 2 Tbsp. (25 mL) butter. Add onion and green pepper
and sauté until tender. Add sauerkraut and corned beef **or** pastrami and
cook until thoroughly heated. Cover and keep warm over low heat.
2. In a bowl, use fork to beat eggs, water, salt and pepper vigorously for
30 seconds.
3. In a well-seasoned 8-inch (20-cm) omelette pan or skillet over medium-
high heat, melt 1 Tbsp. (15 mL) butter until it foams.
4. Pour 1/2 cup (125 mL) egg mixture into pan and allow to set for a few
seconds. Tilt pan and slide rapidly back and forth on the burner, lifting
edges of the omelette with a pancake turner to allow uncooked egg on
top to flow under cooked portion.
5. When top is moist and creamy, add 2 Tbsp. (25 mL) cheese and cook
until cheese begins to melt (about 30 seconds). Omelette should be slightly
brown on the outside, creamy but not liquid on the inside.
6. Split a bread roll and spread with 1 Tbsp. (15 mL) Thousand Island dressing. Roll omelette and turn onto bread roll.
7. Spoon a quarter of the corned beef mixture on top of omelette and serve
immediately. Repeat with remaining ingredients to make 3 more omelettes.

Makes 4 omelettes.

L.A. Smog Omelette

Tiger: *One of the reasons Pat Quinn left town was he couldn't find his way to the Forum.*

2 Tbsp.	butter	25 mL
2 large	red **or** green apples, pared and sliced	2 large
1/2 tsp.	cinnamon	2 mL
8	eggs	8
3 Tbsp.	water	45 mL
1 tsp.	salt	5 mL
1/4 tsp.	pepper	1 mL
4 Tbsp.	butter	60 mL
1/4 lb.	goat cheese, divided in 4 portions	100 g

1. In a skillet over medium-high heat, melt 2 Tbsp. (25 mL) butter and sauté apples until tender (about 10 minutes). Sprinkle with cinnamon, cover, remove from heat and keep warm.
2. In a bowl, use a fork to beat eggs, water, salt and pepper vigorously for 30 seconds.
3. In a well-seasoned 8-inch (20-cm) omelette pan or skillet over medium-high heat, melt 1 Tbsp. (15 mL) butter until it foams.
4. Pour 1/2 cup (125 mL) egg mixture into pan and allow to set for a few seconds. Tilt pan and slide rapidly back and forth on the burner, lifting edges of omelette with a pancake turner to allow uncooked egg on top to flow under cooked portion.
5. When top is moist and creamy, add 1 portion of cheese and cook until cheese begins to melt (about 30 seconds). Top with one quarter of the apple mixture. Omelette should be slightly brown on the outside, creamy but not liquid on the inside. With a spatula, fold in half or fold the sides into the middle. If you fold the omelette in thirds, tilt the pan against a warm serving plate and gently roll the omelette onto it, seam side down. Serve immediately. Repeat with remaining ingredients to make 3 more omelettes.

Makes 4 omelettes.

Edmonton Omelette

Tiger: *This is fast and slick and you can sure get stuffed on it. For the morning after facing the Oilers, the Wurst from the West.*

2 Tbsp.	butter	25 mL
1	garlic clove, minced	1
1/2 cup	chopped onions	125 mL
1/4 cup	chopped green pepper	50 mL
4 drops	Tabasco sauce	4 drops
8 thin slices	kielbasa, diced (see Note)	8 thin slices
8	eggs	8
3 Tbsp.	water	45 mL
1 tsp.	salt	5 mL
1/4 tsp.	pepper	1 mL
4 Tbsp.	butter	60 mL
1/4 cup	sour cream	60 mL
4	French bread rolls	4

1. In a skillet, melt 2 Tbsp. (25 mL) butter. Add garlic, onion and green pepper and sauté until tender. Add Tabasco sauce and kielbasa and cook until thoroughly heated. Cover and keep warm over low heat.
2. In a bowl, use a fork to beat eggs, water, salt and pepper vigorously for 30 seconds.
3. In a well-seasoned 8-inch (20-cm) omelette pan or skillet over medium-high heat, melt 1 Tbsp.(15 mL) butter until it foams.
4. Pour 1/2 cup (125 mL) egg mixture into pan and allow to set for a few seconds. Tilt pan and slide rapidly back and forth on the burner, lifting edges of omelette with a pancake turner to allow uncooked egg on top to flow under cooked portion.
5. When top is moist and creamy, add 1 Tbsp. (15 mL) sour cream and cook 30 seconds. Top omelette with one quarter of kielbasa mixture. Omelette should be slightly brown on the outside, creamy but not liquid on the inside. Roll omelette and turn onto a split French bread roll. Serve immediately. Repeat with remaining ingredients to make 3 more omelettes.

Note: *Kielbasa is a spicy Polish sausage.*

Makes 4 omelettes.

Luc Robitaille's Lasagna Omelette

Tiger: *Inspired by the hotshot L.A. rookie. This is carb-loading at its best.*

8	eggs	8
3 Tbsp.	water	45 mL
1 tsp.	salt	5 mL
1/4 tsp.	pepper	1 mL
4 Tbsp.	butter	60 mL
1/2 cup	grated Mozzarella cheese	100 mL
1/2 cup	cottage cheese	100 mL
1 tsp.	pizza seasoning	5 mL
	salt and pepper to taste	
4 Tbsp.	tomato sauce	60 mL

1. In a bowl, use a fork to beat eggs, water, salt and pepper vigorously for 30 seconds.

2. In a well-seasoned 8-inch (20-cm) omelette pan or skillet over medium-high heat, melt 1 Tbsp. (15 mL) butter until it foams.

3. Pour 1/2 cup (125 mL) egg mixture into pan and allow to set for a few seconds. Tilt pan and slide rapidly back and forth on the burner, lifting edges of omelette with a pancake turner to allow uncooked egg on top to flow under cooked portion.

4. When top is moist and creamy, add 2 Tbsp. (25 mL) Mozzarella cheese and 2 Tbsp. (25 mL) cottage cheese. Cook until cheese begins to melt (about 30 seconds). Add pizza seasoning, salt, pepper and 1 Tbsp. (15 mL) tomato sauce. Omelette should be slightly brown on the outside, creamy but not liquid on the inside. With a spatula, fold in half or fold the sides into the middle. If you fold the omelette in thirds, tilt the pan against a warm serving plate and gently roll the omelette onto it, seam side down. Serve immediately. Repeat with remaining ingredients to make 3 more omelettes.

Makes 4 omelettes.

Philadelphia Cream Cheese and Steak Sandwiches

Tiger: *You could whip the Winnipeg boys and sear the guys from Calgary with this stuff. It gets your juices running. If it's greasy and gooey . . . you've done good!*
Kasey: *A French loaf, sliced lengthwise, filled with thinly sliced steak, cheese, peppers and sauteed onions.*

1/4 cup	olive oil	50 mL
4	green peppers, seeded and quartered	4
1 medium	onion, chopped	1 medium
3	garlic cloves, minced	3
	salt and freshly ground pepper to taste	
8	French bread rolls	8
	Basic Garlic Butter	
8 oz.	whipped cream cheese	250 g
3/4-lb.	sirloin steak, barbecued or broiled to desired degree of doneness	350-g

1. In large skillet, heat olive oil. Add peppers, onion and garlic. Season to taste with salt and pepper. Sauté until vegetables are tender.
2. Halve rolls and brush with Basic Garlic Butter. Place on baking sheet and broil until butter is bubbly and browned. Spread 2 Tbsp. (25 mL) cream cheese on bottom half of each roll.
3. Cut steak into thin slices. Lay a few steak slices on top of cream cheese. Sprinkle with green pepper mixture and top with other half of roll.

Makes 8 sandwiches.

Basic Garlic Butter

1/2 cup	butter	125 mL
2–3	garlic cloves, minced	2–3

Cream butter and add garlic.

Makes 1/2 cup (125 mL).

Washington Capitals Speedy Baked Beans

Tiger: *This has been served on Capitol Hill since Congress began. Now we know why Congress has always failed in the clutch.*
Kasey: *A quick and easy barbecued meat accompaniment.*

1/2 lb.	sliced bacon	250 g
1/4 cup	chopped onion	50 mL
2	celery stalks, chopped	2
1/2 cup	chopped green pepper	125 mL
3–14-oz. cans	pork and beans	3–398-ml cans
1/2 cup	ketchup	125 mL
1 Tbsp.	molasses	15 mL
1 Tbsp.	brown sugar, packed	15 mL
1 tsp.	Tabasco sauce	5 mL
1/4 cup	bacon drippings	50 mL

1. Preheat oven to 375°F (190°C).
2. In a large skillet, fry bacon until almost crisp. Remove bacon and set aside. In bacon drippings, sauté onion, celery and green pepper.
3. In a large, well-greased casserole, combine all ingredients except bacon. Mix well and top with bacon strips.
4. Bake 1 hour.

Makes 12 1/2-cup (125-mL) servings.

Howie Meeker's Barbecued Corn on the Cob with Assorted Butters

Tiger: *I wouldn't let Howie tell me how to describe this, but take it from me—it's great.*
Kasey: *Choose your favourite butter to steam fresh corn on the cob wrapped in foil. Serve remaining butter in bowls alongside.*

12 ears	corn on the cob, husked	12 ears
	corn butters of choice	

Spread 1 Tbsp. (15 mL) corn butter over each cob and wrap securely in double-thickness foil.
To barbecue: Grill 8 inches (20 cm) from coals, turning often until corn is tender when pierced with a fork (about 15 minutes).
To roast: Bake at 375°F (190°C) until tender (about 30 minutes).

Parsley Onion Butter

1/4 cup	butter	50 mL
1 Tbsp.	minced fresh parsley	15 mL
1 Tbsp.	finely minced onion	15 mL
1/4 tsp.	Tiger's Seasoned Salt (page 51)	1 mL

In a medium mixing bowl, beat butter with electric beater until light and fluffy. Beat in parsley, onion and seasoned salt.

Taco Butter

1/4 cup	butter	50 mL
1/4 cup	taco sauce	50 mL
1/2 tsp.	Worcestershire sauce	2 mL
2 dashes	Tabasco sauce	2 dashes
	pinch of ground cumin seed	

In a medium mixing bowl, beat butter with electric beater until light and fluffy. Beat in sauces and cumin.

Garlic Butter

1/4 cup	butter	50 mL
1	garlic clove, minced	1
1 Tbsp.	minced fresh basil	15 mL
1/4 tsp.	Tiger's Seasoned Salt (page 51)	1 mL

In medium mixing bowl, beat butter with electric beater until light and fluffy. Beat in garlic, basil and seasoned salt.

Tiger's Seasoned Salt

2 cups	table salt	500 mL
1 Tbsp.	onion salt	15 mL
2 Tbsp.	celery salt	25 mL
1 Tbsp.	garlic salt	15 mL
2 Tbsp.	paprika	25 mL
1/4 cup	black pepper	50 mL
1/4 cup	white pepper	50 mL
1 Tbsp.	dry mustard	15 mL

Mix all ingredients thoroughly. Store in tightly sealed containers.

Makes about 3 cups (750 mL).

Spuds in Beer

Tiger: *You have to be from Weyburn to appreciate this dish. This is the secret of my success.*
Kasey: *Try these tangy scalloped potatoes with Opponents' Ribs, Eddie Shack's Beer-baked Ham or Rookie's Lamb.*

3 lbs.	potatoes, peeled and thinly sliced	1.5 kg
1 large	onion, thinly sliced	1 large
1/4 cup	flour	50 mL
1-1/2 cups	grated Swiss cheese	375 mL
	salt and freshly ground pepper	
1-1/2 cups	beer	375 mL

1. Preheat oven to 400°F (200°C). Generously butter a 2-1/2 to 3 qt. (2.5–3 L) casserole dish.
2. Arrange one third of the potatoes in casserole dish. Add half the onions and sprinkle with 2 Tbsp. (25 mL) flour. Top with 1/2 cup (125 mL) cheese. Generously sprinkle with salt and pepper.
3. Repeat, using half the remaining potatoes and sprinkling with the remaining onion, remaining 2 Tbsp. (25 mL) flour, and 1/2 cup (125 mL) cheese. Sprinkle with salt and pepper.
4. Spread the remaining potatoes over the top and sprinkle with remaining cheese. Pour in beer.
5. Bake until potatoes are well browned on top and tender when pierced with a fork (about 1–1-1/4 hours).

Serves 4–6.

Opponents' Ribs (p. 74) with Grilled Vegetables (p. 56) and Howie Meeker's Barbecued Corn on the Cob (p. 50-51)

Gordie Howe's Legendary Rice

Tiger: *Legend has it that Gordie raised his kids on this, and I have come to believe this is fact, not fiction.*
Kasey: *You'll love the rich flavour of this buttery rice with rye whiskey . . . suitable for seafood, fish or chicken.*

1/2 cup	butter	125 mL
1 medium	onion, chopped	1 medium
1-1/2 cups	uncooked rice	375 mL
1-3/4 cups	chicken broth	450 mL
1/4 tsp.	salt	1 mL
1/2 cup	rye whiskey	125 mL
3/4 cup	whipping cream	175 mL
1/4 cup	chopped fresh parsley	50 mL
4 Tbsp.	slivered almonds, toasted	50 mL

1. Preheat oven to 350°F (180°C).
2. In 2-qt. (2-L) ovenproof casserole over medium-high heat, melt butter and sauté onion until tender. Stir in rice until well coated with butter. Add chicken broth, salt, rye and whipping cream.
3. Cover and bake until rice is tender (about 40 minutes). Just before serving, add parsley and almonds and fluff with fork.

Serves 6–8.

Tiger's Pizza (p. 64)

Grilled Vegetables with Pesto Mayonnaise

Tiger: *When I barbecue, it's steaks, burgers and salmon. I will have to trust Kasey with this one. Great with Richard Brodeurburgers.*
Kasey: *If no grill or grill pan is available, vegetables may be cooked under the broiler.*

1	eggplant, cut in 10 lengthwise wedges	1
10	whole green onions, unpeeled	10
4	peppers (red, green or yellow), seeded and quartered	4
1	zucchini, cut in 1/2-inch (1.2-cm) diagonal slices	1
3	carrots, sliced diagonally	3
6	whole heads of garlic	6
	olive oil	

1. Coat vegetables lightly with olive oil. Place carrots and garlic directly on the barbecue grill for 5 minutes, then add remaining vegetables. Turn the vegetables as they begin to char and are just tender when tested with a skewer.
2. Spread pesto mayonnaise on a platter about 1/4-inch (7-mm) deep. Arrange vegetables on top. Serve immediately.

Serves 10.

Pesto Mayonnaise

2	garlic cloves	2
2 cups	fresh basil leaves, firmly packed	500 mL
1/2 cup	fresh parsley	125 mL
2 Tbsp.	pine nuts	25 mL
3/4 cup	Parmesan cheese	175 mL
1/2 cup	virgin olive oil	125 mL
3 cups	mayonnaise	750 mL

Combine garlic, basil, parsley, pine nuts and Parmesan cheese in a food processor or blender. Process at high speed, adding oil in small amounts in a slow and steady stream. Place pesto in a bowl and fold in mayonnaise.

Makes 3-1/2 cups (825 mL).

Opposition Puree

Tiger: *Every time Brenda turns on the blender, I think of my opponents and taste this sweet six-carrot victory.*
Kasey: *For a different flavour, you can substitute turnips for the sweet potato.*

6 large	carrots, peeled, cut in 1-1/2-inch (4-cm) slices	6 large
1 large	sweet potato **or** yam, peeled, cut in 3-inch (7.5-cm) pieces	1 large
3 Tbsp.	brown sugar	50 mL
3 Tbsp.	butter	50 mL
3 Tbsp.	sour cream	50 mL
	nutmeg to taste	

1. Preheat oven to 350°F (180°C).
2. Steam carrots and sweet potato **or** yam or boil in salted water until just tender (20–25 minutes). Drain.
3. Process carrots and sweet potato **or** yam in a food processor for 10 seconds. Add sugar, butter, sour cream and nutmeg. Puree 1 minute, stopping to scrape down sides of bowl. Adjust seasoning and spoon into buttered 1-qt. (1-L) casserole dish.
4. Bake 25 minutes or until heated through.

Serves 8–10.

Zucchini à la Zamboni

Tiger: *Just as we clean the ice at the end of the period, we clean up this section of the book.*
Kasey: *A great way to use your bounty of zucchini. Even the kids will eat this.*

3 medium	zucchini,	3 medium
	unpeeled, cut in thin slices	
1/2 cup	sour cream	125 mL
2 Tbsp.	butter	25 mL
2 Tbsp.	grated Monterey Jack **or** cheddar cheese	25 mL
	salt and pepper to taste	
	paprika to taste	
1 Tbsp.	chopped green onions	15 mL
	bread crumbs, butter and	
	grated cheese for topping	

1. Preheat oven to 375°F (190°C).
2. Steam zucchini or cook in small amount of boiling water for 4–6 minutes. Drain zucchini well on paper towels. In a small saucepan, combine sour cream, butter, cheese, salt, pepper and paprika. Stir over low heat until cheese has melted.
3. Remove from heat and mix in green onions. Add zucchini, tossing lightly until well coated. Place in greased 1-qt. (1-L) baking dish. Top with bread crumbs, dot with additional butter and sprinkle with cheese.
4. Bake 15 minutes.

Serves 4.

POWER PLAYS

MAIN DISHES
Power Plays

Referee's Pasta

Tiger: *"Black and white and never right," they say, and we tossed in red salmon to add a bit of colour to this. No fuss, no muss . . .*
Kasey: *. . . You cook the pasta and the sauce in one pot.*

1 cup	whipping cream	250 mL
2 cups	chicken stock	500 mL
1/2 lb.	fresh black fettuccine (squid ink)	250 g
1/2 lb.	fresh egg fettuccine	250 g
1/4 lb.	smoked salmon, sliced	125 g
1-1/4 cups	grated Parmesan cheese	300 mL
	freshly ground pepper	

1. In a large saucepan over medium-high heat, bring cream and chicken stock to a simmer.
2. Rinse fettuccine thoroughly in cold water and drain. Stir fettuccine into cream mixture and cook uncovered until pasta is tender, stirring occasionally. (Once the sauce has returned to the simmer, the pasta will cook in 4–6 minutes.)
3. Add salmon just to heat through. Remove from heat and stir in cheese. Serve immediately with freshly ground pepper.

Serves 4.

Swift Current Casserole
(Deluxe Macaroni and Cheese)

Tiger: *For years I played with this team—it was my life—and after Weyburn it won my heart. I never played better than with a full Swift Current Casserole in my belly.*
Kasey: *No leftovers here.*

2 cups	raw shell macaroni	500 mL
3 Tbsp.	butter	50 mL
3 Tbsp.	flour	50 mL
1 cup	whipping cream	250 mL
1 cup	milk	250 mL
3 Tbsp.	cream cheese, at room temperature	50 mL
2 cups	grated medium cheddar cheese	500 mL
3	green onions, finely chopped	3
1/2	green pepper, chopped	1/2
2	tomatoes, chopped	2
1 tsp.	salt	5 mL

1. Preheat oven to 350°F (180°C).
2. Cook macaroni according to package directions. Rinse in cool water, drain and set aside.
3. Make a white sauce by slowly melting butter in a medium-sized saucepan over medium-low heat. Add flour and stir with a whisk for 3–4 minutes. Gradually add cream and milk and stir until sauce thickens. Stir in cream cheese and 1-1/2 cups (375 mL) cheddar cheese just until blended.
4. Remove from heat and add onions, green pepper, tomatoes, salt and macaroni. Turn mixture into a greased 13 × 9 inch (4-L) ovenproof casserole dish. Sprinkle with remaining 1/2 cup (125 mL) grated cheddar cheese.
5. Bake 30 minutes.

Serves 6–8.

Italian Sausage Pasta

Tiger: *From Vancouver to New York, everyone will want to try this hearty pasta dish.*
Kasey: *And everyone will rave about it.*

1-1/2 lbs.	chorizo sausage	750 g
1/2 cup	olive oil	125 mL
1 large	eggplant, about 1-1/2 lbs. (750 g), cut in 1-inch (2.5-cm) cubes	1 large
1 large	onion, chopped	1 large
1	green pepper, chopped	1
3 large	garlic cloves, minced	3 large
1 tsp. each	oregano, basil and thyme	5 mL each
1 tsp.	sugar	5 mL
	salt and freshly ground pepper to taste	
2–14-oz. cans	Italian plum tomatoes	2–398-mL cans
1/4 cup	coarsely chopped stuffed green olives	50 mL
1 cup	dry red wine	250 mL
1-1/2 lbs.	dried rotini or large shell pasta	750 g
1 cup	freshly grated Parmesan cheese	250 mL
1/4 cup	chopped fresh parsley	50 mL

1. Remove casings from sausage. In a heavy pot, brown sausage until crumbly. Drain and transfer to a bowl.
2. Heat oil in the same pot. Sauté eggplant, onion, green pepper, garlic, oregano, basil, thyme, sugar, salt and pepper.
3. When eggplant is soft, add sausage, tomatoes and olives. Bring to a boil, reduce heat and simmer about 1-1/2 hours, stirring occasionally until sauce is thickened. Add wine and salt and pepper to taste.
4. Serve over your choice of hot pasta and sprinkle with Parmesan cheese and parsley.

Serves 8.

Tiger's Pizza

Tiger: *Hey, what can I say?*
Kasey: *To simulate a pizza oven, line your oven rack with unglazed quarry tiles or a baking stone. Always preheat oven for at least 30 minutes.*

3 cups	unbleached flour	750 mL
1 Tbsp.	dry yeast	15 mL
1/2 cup	warm water	125 mL
	(105°–115°F/41°–46°C)	
1 cup	warm milk	250 mL
2 Tbsp.	olive oil	25 mL
1-1/2 tsp.	salt	7 mL

Pizza Dough

1. Measure flour into a large mixing bowl or food processor.
2. In a small bowl, sprinkle yeast into warm water and let stand until foamy and dissolved (about 10 minutes).
3. If mixing by hand, make a well in the centre of the flour, pour in dissolved yeast mixture, add warm milk and stir with a wooden spoon. Add olive oil and salt, mixing until well combined. Turn dough out onto a lightly floured surface and knead gently until it is smooth and satiny, about 10 minutes.
If using a food processor, turn machine on and pour yeast mixture and warm milk through the feed tube. Process until a ball of dough forms, then add the oil and process until smooth (about 40 seconds). Turn dough out onto a lightly floured surface.
4. Cover with a mixing bowl and let rise until doubled in volume (2-1/2–3 hours).
5. Punch down dough and knead several times. Divide into 3 pieces. Form the pieces into balls and flour lightly. Cover with a towel and let balls rise (about 10 minutes). (At this point, dough may be refrigerated for 3 days or frozen. Bring to room temperature before proceeding.)

Assembly

1. Preheat oven to 450°F (230°C).
2. Lightly sprinkle a heavy pizza pan or baking pan with cornmeal. Press the dough into a flat disc and then roll or stretch dough into 3 rounds, 11 inches (28 cm) in diameter, leaving the edges thicker.
3. Brush lightly with olive oil to help keep bottom crisp.
4. Spread pizza sauce, if desired, on each round. Add desired toppings from Crustless Pizza (page 14).

Makes 3 pizzas.

Beer Fritter Batter

Tiger: *I'm never one to waste beer. Kasey swung me over to this title and to the food . . . the best batter ever.*
Kasey: *Use this tender batter to coat shellfish, fish and vegetables—or any other favourites you wish to deep-fry.*

1 cup	flour	250 mL
1/4 tsp.	salt	1 mL
1 cup	flat beer	250 mL
2 Tbsp.	olive oil	25 mL
2	egg whites	2
	onions	
	zucchini, cut in 1/3-inch (6-mm) diagonal slices	
	clams	
	fish fillets	
	oysters	
	prawns	

1. In a medium bowl, combine flour and salt. Make a well in centre and pour in beer and oil. With an electric beater, beat until very smooth. Let stand at least 1 hour.
2. In a small bowl, beat egg whites until stiff. Stir beer batter and fold in beaten egg whites.
3. Dip prepared vegetables or fish into batter; let excess drip back into bowl. Deep-fry in hot oil (375°F/190°C) until golden brown. When deep-frying, never fill pot more than halfway with oil; or use electric deep-fryer. Drain on paper towels and serve warm.

Makes about 2 cups (500 mL) batter, enough for 3–4 servings.

New York Chicken Burger

Tiger: *It's probably one name I'll regret if I'm traded there, but then again there is not a better recipe in this book.*
Kasey: *This tender breast of chicken is my idea of a perfect hamburger.*

6	bacon slices	6
1 Tbsp.	butter	15 mL
2 Tbsp.	oil	25 mL
2	whole chicken breasts, halved, boned and skinned	2
4	onion cheese buns	4
4 slices	Swiss cheese	4 slices
4 slices	tomato	4 slices

1. Cut bacon slices in half and fry until crisp. Drain and set aside.
2. In a skillet over medium-high heat, melt butter with oil and sauté chicken breasts 5 minutes on each side.
3. Meanwhile, butter the buns. Sauté them in a separate skillet, using a weight to flatten them.
4. During last minute of cooking, top each chicken breast with a slice of cheese; cover skillet with foil until cheese melts. Remove from heat. Place chicken breasts on onion buns and top with 3 pieces of bacon and a slice of tomato. Serve immediately.

Makes 4 burgers.

Stan Smyl's Captain's Dish

Tiger: *For a stand-up guy who always kept the team on course. I thought I would name this recipe after him as it, too, gives a solid performance.*
Kasey: *This tangy dish may be prepared in advance and refrigerated.*

3-lb.	chicken, cut in 8 pieces	1.5-kg
1/4 cup	flour	50 mL
	salt and freshly ground pepper	
2 Tbsp.	butter	25 mL
1 Tbsp.	olive oil	15 mL
1 large	onion, sliced	1 large
1	green pepper, diced	1
1	garlic clove, minced	1
1-1/2 Tbsp.	curry powder	20 mL
1/4 tsp.	thyme	1 mL
1/4 tsp.	mace **or** nutmeg	1 mL
28-oz. can	stewed tomatoes	796-mL can
1/2 tsp.	Tabasco sauce	2 mL
1/2 cup	raisins	125 mL
1/2 cup	slivered almonds, toasted **(optional)**	125 mL
4 cups	cooked rice	1 L

1. Combine flour, salt and pepper. Dredge chicken pieces lightly in the seasoned flour.
2. In a large skillet over medium-high heat, melt butter and add oil. Add chicken pieces without crowding and brown on all sides. Remove and set aside.
3. Add onion, green pepper, garlic, curry, thyme and mace **or** nutmeg and sauté until vegetables are just tender. Stir in tomatoes and Tabasco sauce. Return chicken to the skillet. Cover and simmer until chicken is tender (about 25 minutes). Add raisins and almonds and simmer 5 minutes. Serve over cooked rice.

Serves 4–6.

Richard Brodeurburgers

Tiger: *Every goalie has a secret. Success doesn't come easy when you are the one in the net, but Brodeur always makes it look easy. I call this after him because it looks easy too.*
Kasey: *Do not overcook these burgers or they will end up looking (and tasting) like pucks.*

2-1/2 lbs.	ground beef	1.25 kg
1/2 cup	chili sauce	125 mL
3/4 cup	finely chopped onions	175 mL
2 Tbsp.	finely chopped green peppers	25 mL
1 Tbsp.	horseradish	15 mL
1 Tbsp.	Worcestershire sauce	15 mL
1/4 tsp.	pepper	1 mL
8	hamburger buns **or** Kaiser rolls	8
	lettuce and tomato for garnish	

1. Combine all ingredients except buns and garnishes, mixing lightly until ingredients are evenly distributed.
2. Shape into 8 patties, 3/4 inch (2 cm) thick. Place on grill or on rack in broiler pan, 3 – 4 inches (7.5 – 10 cm) from heat. Broil 7 – 8 minutes on first side, turn and broil 6 – 8 minutes or until cooked as desired. Serve on hamburger buns or split Kaiser rolls with lettuce, tomato and Onion Mayonnaise Topping.

Makes 8 burgers.

Onion Mayonnaise Topping

1 cup	mayonnaise	250 mL
1 cup	sour cream	250 mL
1/2 cup	chopped green onions	125 mL
2 Tbsp.	lemon juice	25 mL

Combine all ingredients and mix well. Store in refrigerator.

Makes 2 cups (500 mL).

Smythe Division Burger

Substitute cooked sliced mushrooms for tomato. Combine 1 cup (250 mL) Onion Mayonnaise Topping with 1/4 cup (50 mL) chopped red pepper and 1 Tbsp. (15 mL) horseradish.

Norris Division Burger

Substitute sliced peaches for tomato. Combine 1 cup (250 mL) Onion Mayonnaise Topping with 1/3 cup (75 mL) chopped peanuts.

Patrick Division Burger

Substitute sliced avocado for tomato. Combine 1 cup (250 mL) Onion Mayonnaise Topping with 1/4 cup (50 mL) chopped green pepper and 1/2 tsp.
(2 mL) chili powder.

Adams Division Burger

Before cooking, wrap a bacon slice around each burger; secure with toothpicks. Combine 1 cup (250 mL) Onion Mayonnaise Topping with 3/4 cup (175 mL) shredded cheddar cheese and 1 Tbsp. (15 mL) steak sauce.

Coach's Dilemma Chili-Mac

Tiger: *It's never easy for these guys to make the tough decisions, so I solved this dilemma with a sure-win solution.*
Kasey: *Chili is personal—feel free to add ingredients or change quantities.*

2 Tbsp.	peanut oil	25 mL
2 large	garlic cloves, minced	2 large
1 cup	chopped onion	250 mL
1	green pepper, seeded and chopped	1
2 lbs.	ground beef	1 kg
2–48-oz. cans	stewed tomatoes	2–1.36-L cans
2–14-oz. cans	red kidney beans	2–398-mL cans
1 cup	uncooked macaroni	250 mL
3 Tbsp.	chili powder	50 mL

1. In a large saucepan, heat oil and add garlic, onion and green pepper. Cook, stirring, until vegetables are wilted (about 3 minutes).
2. Add beef and stir to break up lumps. Cook until meat loses its red colour. Add tomatoes, kidney beans, macaroni and chili powder and simmer 30 minutes.
3. Serve in bowls with any of the following: grated Monterey Jack, cheddar or Mozzarella cheese; chopped green onions; sour cream; crushed red pepper flakes.

Serves 12.

New York Chicken Burger (p. 66), Defensive Salad (p. 34) and beer

Bag-a-Steak

Tiger: *Fans of certain teams have been known to come to the rink wearing bags on their heads. Why can't a steak wear one?*
Kasey: *Great with Spuds in Beer or served with breads, mustards and pickles.*

3-lb.	sirloin, 2 inches (7.5 cm) thick, at room temperature	1.5 kg
	olive oil	
1/4 cup	butter	50 mL
2	garlic cloves, minced	2
2 tsp.	Tiger's Seasoned Salt (page 51)	10 mL
2 tsp.	seasoned pepper	10 mL

1. Preheat oven to 375°F (190°C).
2. Rub oil on both sides of steak. Mix together butter, garlic, seasoned salt and pepper. Spread on both sides of steak. Place steak in a brown paper bag, seal tightly and place on a baking sheet. Insert a meat thermometer through bag into centre of meat.
3. For rare meat, bake 40–45 minutes (140°F/60°C on meat thermometer). For medium, bake 10 minutes longer (160°F/70°C). For well done, bake 5 minutes longer (170°F/75°C). Remove steak from bag and carve diagonally in thin slices.

Serves 4–6.

Bantam Turkey Chili with garnishes (p. 81), Portuguese buns and beer

Opponents' Ribs

Tiger: *Take two—or four for that matter—and break gently. This is a favourite of coaches and policemen alike. I love it—and I'm no coach!*
Kasey: *Tender meat, slippery sauce and crunchy bones always hold appeal. These ribs will guarantee your reputation.*

To barbecue spareribs, first parboil briefly to eliminate some of the fat that flares up if it drips on the coals. Parboiling also helps tenderize the meat. When the cooking meat starts to sizzle, turn the ribs; let them come to a sizzle on the other side and then turn again. Turn them often so sauce does not burn.

4 lbs.	spareribs	2 kg
	salt and pepper to taste	
1/2 cup	ketchup	125 mL
1/2 cup	soy sauce	125 mL
1/4 cup	orange juice	50 mL
2 Tbsp.	lemon juice	25 mL
2 Tbsp.	grated orange peel	25 mL
2 large	garlic cloves, minced	2 large
2 Tbsp.	minced ginger root	25 mL
1 cup	brown sugar	250 mL
2 Tbsp.	orange flavoured liqueur	25 mL

1. Preheat oven to 350°F (180°C).
2. Season ribs to taste with salt and pepper. Lay in roasting pan, cover with foil and bake for 1 hour.
3. Meanwhile, combine remaining ingredients and stir to mix well.
4. Remove roasting pan from oven and pour orange barbecue sauce over ribs. Bake uncovered 30 minutes or until ribs are tender.

Serves 4–6.

Roast Pork Loin with Red Currant Sauce

Tiger: *You wouldn't believe my first draft comments on this recipe of Kasey's so I'm only going to tell you that the interpreters got the better of me. So just enjoy it.*
Kasey: *This is a superb recipe and a breeze to prepare for special guests.*

1	pork loin roast, 5–6 lbs. (2.25–2.75 kg)	1
1	garlic clove	1
	salt and pepper to taste	
	Red Currant Sauce	

1. Preheat oven to 325°F (160°C).
2. Rub roast with garlic clove and season with salt and pepper. Place fat side up on rack in low-sided open pan. Insert meat thermometer into centre of roast, making sure the tip does not touch any bone. Roast for 2-1/2 hours.
3. Meanwhile, prepare Red Currant Sauce.
4. Remove roast from oven and baste with Red Currant Sauce. Return to oven until meat thermometer reads 170°F (80°C), 15–30 minutes. Serve with remaining sauce on side.

Serves 8–10.

Red Currant Sauce

1 Tbsp.	vegetable oil	15 mL
1/3 cup	finely chopped onion	75 mL
10-oz. jar	red currant jelly	284-mL jar
3/4 cup	chili sauce	175 mL
2 Tbsp.	lemon juice	25 mL
1/4 cup	apple jelly	50 mL
2 Tbsp.	dry white wine	25 mL

In medium saucepan, heat oil and sauté onion until tender. Add remaining ingredients and simmer 30 minutes or until mixture reduces to 1-1/2 cups (375 mL).

Habs Tourtiere

Tiger: *This meal is so hefty and famous that they named a team after it. I'm not much on accents except my own, but Kasey says "Tourtiere" is pronounced more or less like it reads.*
Kasey: *This traditional meat pie continues to be a mainstay of French Canadian cooking. Serve with crisp vegetables and a bottle of sturdy red wine.*

Sour Cream Pastry

2 cups	flour	500 mL
1 cup	butter, in 4 equal portions	250 mL
1/2 cup	sour cream	125 mL
1	egg yolk	1

1. Place flour in bowl of food processor. Distribute butter evenly over flour. Process until well blended. In a small bowl, mix sour cream and egg yolk and add to flour-butter mixture. Process until well incorporated.
2. Remove to lightly floured work surface and shape into a flat disc. Cover with plastic wrap and chill 1 hour or until pastry is firm enough to roll out.

Makes enough for 1 large double-crust pie.

Filling

2 Tbsp.	butter	25 mL
1 medium	onion, chopped	1 medium
2	garlic cloves, minced	2
1	celery stalk, diced	1
1 lb.	ground pork	500 g
1/2 lb.	ground veal	250 g
3/4 cup	hot water	175 mL
1/4 tsp.	pepper, or to taste	1 mL
1/2 tsp.	cinnamon	2 mL
1/4 tsp.	cloves	1 mL
1/2 tsp.	savory	2 mL

In a large skillet over medium-high heat, melt butter. Add onions, garlic and celery and sauté until tender. Add meat and water and simmer 30 minutes. Add seasonings, stir well and simmer 5 minutes. Cool.

Assembly

1. Preheat oven to 450°F (230°C).

2. Roll out half of pastry dough and line a 10-inch (25-cm) pie plate. Spoon filling onto bottom crust.

3. Roll out remaining dough for top crust. Place over the filling and press all around the outer edges to seal. Cut slits in pastry to allow steam to escape.

4. Bake until crust is golden (15–20 minutes). Reduce heat to 325°F (160°C) and bake 30 minutes more.

Serves 6–8.

Corn Dogs

Tiger: *Being from Saskatchewan, I know all about this recipe first hand. You don't mess with corn dogs like you don't mess with the Prairie hockey players. They even love this in L.A.*

Kasey: *These also make delicious appetizers when cut in 1-inch (2.5-cm) pieces and served with a variety of mustards.*

1/2 cup	cornmeal	125 mL
1-1/2 cups	flour	375 mL
1/4 cup	sugar	50 mL
1/4 tsp.	pepper	1 mL
2 tsp.	salt	10 mL
4 tsp.	baking powder	20 mL
1	egg	1
1 cup	milk	250 mL
1 lb.	wieners	500 g

1. Mix together cornmeal, flour, sugar, pepper, salt and baking powder. Beat egg and add milk. Beat with electric beater until smooth.

2. Dip wieners in batter and deep-fry in hot, deep oil (375°F/190°C) or in deep-fryer until brown on one side. Turn and brown on the other side. Drain on paper towels. Serve hot with mustard.

Serves 8–10.

Orange-glazed Ham Loaf

Tiger: *Loafers and hams have always been floaters to me. So add orange glaze and you are all set.*
Kasey: *Not your ordinary meatloaf.*

1-1/2 cups	soft bread crumbs	375 mL
1/3 cup	orange juice	75 mL
2 Tbsp.	lemon juice	25 mL
1 lb.	ground ham	500 g
1 lb.	ground pork	500 g
1/4 cup	chopped onion	50 mL
2 Tbsp.	freshly chopped parsley	25 mL
2	eggs, lightly beaten	2
1/4 cup	brown sugar	50 mL
1/2 tsp.	dry mustard	2 mL
1 tsp.	flour	5 mL

1. Preheat oven to 350°F (180°C).
2. Place bread crumbs in a large mixing bowl. Mix orange and lemon juices and pour over bread crumbs. Add ham, pork, onion, parsley and eggs and mix gently but thoroughly.
3. Mix together brown sugar, mustard and flour. Sprinkle evenly in bottom of greased 9 × 5 inch (2-L) loaf pan. Press meat mixture over brown sugar mixture. Bake uncovered 45 minutes.
4. Prepare Orange Glaze. Pour about 1/4 cup (50 mL) Orange Glaze evenly over loaf and bake another 30 minutes. Turn upside down on serving platter. Slice. Serve with remaining hot Orange Glaze.

Serves 8.

Orange Glaze

1 Tbsp.	cornstarch	15 mL
1/4 cup	sugar	50 mL
1-1/2 cups	orange juice	375 mL
	dash of salt	

In a saucepan, combine cornstarch and sugar. Stir in orange juice and salt. Stir over medium-high heat until mixture boils and thickens.

Rookie's Lamb

Tiger: *My grandfather said you may as well get hung for sheep as lamb. In fact, so did my dad and brothers. At any rate, this is a recipe for both sheep and lamb, but rookies seldom follow . . . so it's rookie lamb.*
Kasey: *Rookie's Lamb is tender and young and a breeze to carve.*

3-lb.	butterflied leg of lamb	1.5-kg
1/3 cup	lemon juice	75 mL
1/4 cup	Dijon mustard	50 mL
3/4 cup	olive oil	175 mL
3 large	garlic cloves	3 large
1 Tbsp.	tarragon	15 mL
3 Tbsp.	chopped fresh parsley	50 mL
	salt and freshly ground pepper to taste	

1. Place lamb in a strong plastic bag. Combine remaining ingredients and pour over lamb. Marinate several hours or overnight. Remove from refrigerator 1 hour before cooking.
2. To broil: Set oven broiler to high. Transfer lamb to a shallow roasting pan. Broil 4–6 inches (10–15 cm) from heat for 12–15 minutes on each side.
To barbecue: Place lamb on an oiled grill about 4 inches (10 cm) from coals. Barbecue 10–12 minutes on each side for medium-rare meat.
3. Slice lamb diagonally across the grain and serve immediately.

Serves 6–8.

Stickhandler's Shish Kebab

Tiger: *Some of us need to skewer other teams while one of us out-stickhandles the rest. I added a bit of booze just to set the tone for this recipe.*
Kasey: *Salmon and shrimps for your special guests . . . ideal for the first spring barbecue.*

1-1/2 lbs.	salmon, skinned and boned	750 g
1/2 lb	medium shrimp, shelled and deveined	250 g
8	bacon slices, cut in halves	8
2 small	zucchini, cut in 1/4-inch (5-mm) slices	2 small
1/2 lb.	fresh mushrooms, stems removed	250 g
2 cups	cherry tomatoes	500 mL
1 large	green pepper, seeded, cut in 1-inch (2.5-cm) squares	1 large
Marinade		
1/2 cup	dry sherry	125 mL
3 Tbsp.	lemon juice	50 mL
2 Tbsp.	soy sauce	25 mL
2 Tbsp.	olive oil	25 mL
1 Tbsp.	honey	15 mL
1 tsp.	lemon rind	5 mL
1 large	garlic clove, minced	1 large
1 tsp.	ground ginger	5 mL

1. Soak 8 wooden skewers in cold water for at least 1 hour.
2. Cut salmon into 1-1/2-inch (4-cm) cubes.
3. With paper towel, pat shrimp dry.
4. Heat a skillet over medium-high heat. Add bacon and cook 1 minute. Drain off and reserve the bacon fat. Cook bacon a further 2 minutes, until partly cooked. Drain and set aside.
5. Combine all marinade ingredients in a bowl and add reserved bacon fat. Whisk to blend. Add salmon, shrimp and vegetables and gently mix to coat with marinade. Cover with plastic wrap and refrigerate for 30 minutes.
6. Drain salmon, shrimp and vegetables over a bowl. Reserve the marinade.
7. Thread salmon, shrimp, vegetables and bacon on wooden skewers. (Kebabs may be refrigerated, covered, at this point. Bring to room temperature before cooking.)

8. To broil: Set oven broiler to high. Place kebabs 4 inches (10 cm) from heat for 3–5 minutes on each side, basting with reserved marinade.

 To barbecue: Place kebabs on the grill 6 inches (15 cm) from coals. Barbecue 3–5 minutes on each side, basting with reserved marinade.

Makes 8 kebabs.

Bantam Turkey Chili

Tiger: *Need I say more . . .*
Kasey: *Like all well-seasoned dishes, this tastes better the second day.*

1 cup	chopped onions	250 mL
1 cup	chopped green pepper	250 mL
2 large	garlic cloves, minced	2 large
3 Tbsp.	vegetable oil	50 mL
2–14-oz. cans	stewed tomatoes	2–398-ml cans
2–14-oz. cans	kidney beans	2–398-ml cans
1 cup	dry red wine	250 mL
4 cups	cooked turkey, cut in bite-sized pieces	1 L
2 Tbsp.	chili powder	25 mL
1 tsp.	crushed red pepper flakes	5 mL
1 tsp.	salt	5 mL

1. In a medium-large saucepan, sauté onions, green pepper and garlic in oil until tender. Add remaining ingredients and simmer 30 minutes.
2. Serve with garnishes such as grated Monterey Jack, cheddar or Mozzarella cheese; chopped green onions; sour cream; crushed red pepper flakes.

Serves 6.

Eddie Shack's Beer-baked Ham

Tiger: *Eddie used to stick his nose into everything, so when he wanted to stick it in my book, I named this recipe after him.*
Kasey: *Beer-baked Ham is also delicious served cold and thinly sliced.*

6–7 lbs.	boneless hostess ham	2.75–3.25 kg
	whole cloves	
1 Tbsp.	dry mustard	15 mL
2/3 cup	molasses	175 mL
2 cups	beer	500 mL
3 Tbsp.	cornstarch	50 mL
1/2 cup	cold water	125 mL
2 Tbsp.	lemon juice	25 mL
3 Tbsp.	ground ginger	50 mL
1 cup	raisins,	250 mL
	soaked in hot water until plump	

1. Preheat oven to 350°F (180°C).
2. Score ham diagonally to form 1-inch (2.5-cm) diamonds. Stud with cloves. Combine mustard and molasses and spread over ham. Place ham in roasting pan and roast for 1 hour, basting with beer every 10 minutes. Remove ham from oven and keep warm.
3. Cook pan juices in roasting pan until reduced to 2 cups (500 mL). Blend cornstarch with cold water and add to pan juices, stirring until thickened and smooth. Add lemon juice and ginger and simmer several minutes. Just before serving, stir in raisins. Pour into serving dish.

Serves 15–20.

Tiger's Prawns

Tiger: *What can you say? I have had a hell of a time with this recipe but now we've sorted it all out. It wasn't my idea because I don't have Pernod in my bar (beer yes, Pernod no), so we made it an optional ingredient for the downtown crowd.*

Kasey: *The prawns may be served peeled or with the shells on. Serve with crusty bread as a first course or with pasta as a main course.*

4 Tbsp.	butter	50 mL
3	garlic cloves, minced	3
1-1/2 lbs.	prawns, tails attached, heads and shells removed	750 g
1	jalapeño pepper, chopped **or**	1
1/4 tsp.	crushed red pepper	1 mL
2 Tbsp.	white wine	25 mL
2 Tbsp.	Pernod **or**	25 mL
1/4 tsp.	anise seed, crushed	1 mL
	juice of 1 lime	
2 Tbsp.	finely chopped fresh parsley	25 mL

1. In a large skillet over medium-high heat, melt butter. Add garlic and sauté 10 seconds. Add prawns and pepper and sauté until prawns turn opaque white (about 2 minutes). Remove from heat.

2. Add wine, Pernod **or** anise seed, and lime juice. Return to heat just until prawns are cooked (about 2 minutes). Serve immediately, sprinkled with parsley.

Serves 4–6.

PLAYOFFS

DESSERTS
Playoffs

Stanley (Peanut Butter) Cup Bars

Tiger: *The ultimate cup bars for the ultimate trophy. Teams will fight for these bars like they fight for the Cup. Anyhow, peanut butter is good for you.*
Kasey: *Our version of that favourite combination of the chocolate and peanut butter candy.*

2 cups	semisweet chocolate chips	500 mL
1 cup	peanut butter	250 mL
1 cup	chopped peanuts	250 mL
1-1/2 cups	Graham wafer crumbs	375 mL
1 cup	butter, melted	250 mL
3 cups	sifted icing sugar	750 mL

1. Melt chocolate chips in a double boiler over warm (not hot) water. Stir once when melted.
2. Meanwhile, combine remaining ingredients and press evenly into a 13 × 9 inch (4-L) baking pan. Spread melted chocolate over peanut base. Cool, cut into 2-in. (5-cm) squares and place in refrigerator. These bars may be frozen.

Makes 24 bars.

Turtle Bars

Tiger: *There is only one way to better a turtle, and that is to add a whipping!*
Kasey: *Our homemade version of one of the most popular chocolates sold.*

Bottom Layer

2 cups	flour	500 mL
1 cup	brown sugar	250 mL
1/2 cup	butter	125 mL
1-1/2 cups	pecan halves	375 mL

Topping

1/2 cup	brown sugar	125 mL
2/3 cup	butter	150 mL
2 cups	chocolate chips	500 mL

1. Preheat oven to 350°F (180°C).
2. Combine flour, sugar and butter until mixture has consistency of coarse crumbs. Press into ungreased 13 × 9 inch (4-L) baking pan. Sprinkle evenly with pecans.
3. In a small saucepan, combine 1/2 cup (125 mL) sugar and 2/3 cup (150 mL) butter. Stir constantly over medium-high heat until mixture begins to boil. Boil 1 minute. Pour over pecans.
4. Bake until firm (20–25 minutes). Remove from oven and cover evenly with chocolate chips. Cool completely on wire rack and cut into 2-in. (5-cm) squares.

Makes 24 bars.

Butter Tarts

Tiger: *In every good cookbook there's a recipe that's rich and gooey and almost too close to home cooking. Leaving home was never as tough as leaving Mom's butter tarts.*
Kasey: *These melt-in-your-mouth tarts are perennial favourites on the Prairies.*

1/4 cup	butter, at room temperature	50 mL
1 cup	brown sugar	250 mL
2	eggs	2
1 tsp.	vanilla extract	5 mL
2 Tbsp.	water	25 mL
1/3 cup	raisins	75 mL
24–36	unbaked tart shells	24–36

1. Preheat oven to 375°F (190°C).
2. Blend butter and sugar. Add eggs, vanilla and water; mix well. Sprinkle a few raisins on bottom of tart shells. Pour in the filling. Bake 10 minutes. Reduce heat to 350°F (180°C) and bake until pastry is browned (about 10 minutes). Cool before removing from pans.

Makes 2–3 dozen.

Maple Leaf Apple Brownies

Tiger: *We put these two recipes together because you can't have one without the other. If you make it through this page, you will accumulate calories like I accumulated penalty minutes while I was on this team. Hope you have as much fun as I did!*
Kasey: *These moist brownies are filled with chunks of apple, spiced with cinnamon, allspice and cloves and topped with maple cream.*

1/4 cup	butter	50 mL
1 cup	brown sugar	250 mL
1	egg	1
2 cups	peeled, cored and diced apples	500 mL
1 cup	self-raising flour	250 mL
1/2 tsp.	cinnamon	2 mL
1/2 tsp.	allspice	2 mL
1/4 tsp.	ground cloves	1 mL
1/2 cup	chopped pecans	125 mL
1/4 cup	icing sugar (**optional**)	50 mL

1. Preheat oven to 350°F (180°C).
2. Cream butter. Gradually beat in sugar until light and fluffy. Add eggs, one at a time, beating after each. Add apples.
3. Combine flour and spices. Add to apple mixture and combine thoroughly. Fold in pecans.
4. Pour into a greased 9 × 9 inch (2.5-L) pan and bake 30 minutes. Cool. Sprinkle with icing sugar or serve with Maple Leaf Cream.

Maple Leaf Cream

1 cup	maple syrup	250 mL
1/2 cup	water	125 mL
1 Tbsp.	butter	15 mL
2 tsp.	flour	10 mL
1/2 cup	light cream	125 mL
1 cup	whipping cream	250 mL

1. In a small saucepan, combine syrup and juice. Boil down to 3/4 cup (200 mL) (about 15 minutes).
2. Melt butter in a wide 2-qt. (2-L) saucepan. Blend in flour and cream. Blend in reduced syrup. Boil, uncovered, until reduced to 1 cup (250 mL) (about 10 minutes). Cool.
3. While mixture cools, whip cream. Fold whipped cream into cool mixture.

Makes 1-1/2 cups (375 mL).

Fans' Jam Tarts

Tiger: *The editors told me that I can't call any player a jam tart and you can't call a whole team a serving of jam tarts . . . so that just leaves me with the fans who have always been good to me. But then again, there have been one or two . . .*
Kasey: *Count on seconds and thirds with these tarts.*

1 cup	butter	250 mL
8 oz.	cream cheese	250 g
2 cups	all purpose flour	500 mL
	dash of salt	
3 Tbsp.	sugar	50 mL
1/2 cup	jam **or** marmalade	125 mL
	icing sugar	

1. Preheat oven to 325°F (160°C).
2. With pastry blender or in food processor, blend butter, cream cheese, flour, salt and sugar. Chill 1 hour.
3. Roll dough 1/8 inch (3 mm) thick on generously floured work surface. Cut into 3-inch (7.5-cm) circles. Spoon 1 tsp. (5 mL) jam **or** marmalade on one half of each circle. Fold dough over filling and press edges together.
4. Place tarts 1 inch (2.5 cm) apart on ungreased baking sheet and refrigerate 10 minutes. Bake 10–15 minutes or until lightly browned. Cool. Dust with icing sugar before serving.

Makes 2 dozen.

Chris Nilan's Pound Cake

Tiger: *You only put this out if you need protection—even in Montreal they remember this for entertaining out-of-town guests.*
Kasey: *This is a surprisingly moist cake.*

3 cups	sugar	750 mL
1 cup	butter	250 mL
6	eggs, separated	6
3 cups	self-raising flour	750 mL
1 cup	sour cream	250 mL
1 tsp.	vanilla extract	5 mL
1 tsp.	almond extract	5 mL
1 tsp.	lemon extract	5 mL

1. Preheat oven to 350°F (180°C).
2. Cream sugar and butter until very creamy. Add egg yolks one at a time, beating well with electric beater after each addition. Add flour and sour cream alternately. Blend well. Add flavourings.
3. Beat egg whites until stiff and fold into batter. Pour into well-greased, lightly floured tube pan or loaf pan. Bake 1-1/2 hours or until cake tests done. Cool in pan 10 minutes. Turn out and pour Lemon Glaze over hot cake.

Lemon Glaze

1-1/2 cups	icing sugar	375 mL
1/4 cup	fresh lemon juice	50 mL

Mix together sugar and lemon juice. Pour over hot cake.

Funeral Pie

Tiger: *This is the last minute of play. It sure looked like I would need this when Detroit sent me down, but I didn't find it till now so it nearly ends the book—not my career.*

Kasey: *An easy and different approach to raisin pie.*

	Sour Cream Pastry (page 76)	
2 cups	raisins	500 mL
1 cup	orange juice	250 mL
1 cup	water	250 mL
1 tsp.	grated orange peel	5 mL
3/4 cup	sugar	175 mL
2 Tbsp.	cornstarch	25 mL
3/4 tsp.	ground allspice	3 mL
1/8 tsp.	freshly grated nutmeg	0.5 mL
1 Tbsp.	lemon juice	15 mL
1/2 cup	chopped walnuts	125 mL
1	egg, beaten	1
1 Tbsp.	sugar	15 mL
	whipped cream **or** vanilla ice cream	

1. Preheat oven to 425°F (220°C).

2. Prepare Sour Cream Pastry. Roll out one half and line a 10-inch (25-cm) pie plate. Set aside in cool place. Refrigerate remaining pastry.

3. In medium saucepan, bring raisins, orange juice, water and orange peel to boil. Boil 5 minutes.

4. Meanwhile, in small bowl combine 3/4 cup (175 mL) sugar, cornstarch, allspice and nutmeg. Stir into raisin mixture. Cook until thickened (about 2 minutes). Add lemon juice and walnuts. Pour into pie shell.

5. Roll out remaining dough and cover pie. Trim and flute edges. Cut slits in top of pie to allow steam to escape. Brush with beaten egg and sprinkle with 1 Tbsp. (15 mL) sugar.

6. Bake until golden brown (20–25 minutes). Serve slightly warm with whipped cream or ice cream.

Serves 8.

King Clancy Hall of Fame Cheesecake

Tiger: *This started out as just the Hall of Fame but there are few more deserving of the tie-in than the King—who made the Hall of Fame as this recipe will make any cookbook Hall of Fame.*
Kasey: *For the children in all of us.*

Cookie Crumb Crust

20	Oreo chocolate cookies, finely crushed	20
6 Tbsp.	unsalted butter, melted	100 mL
1/4 cup	sugar	50 mL

1. In a mixing bowl, thoroughly blend Oreo cookie crumbs, butter and sugar.
2. Press crumb mixture evenly into a greased 9-inch (2.5-L) springform pan. Chill.

Filling

15	Oreo chocolate cookies	15
2 lbs.	cream cheese, at room temperature	1 kg
1-1/2 cups	sugar	375 mL
6	eggs	6
1 Tbsp.	rum	15 mL

1. Break cookies into large pieces.
2. In a large bowl, beat cream cheese with electric beater at medium speed until smooth. Gradually add sugar and eggs, beating after each addition. Stir in rum. Carefully fold in broken cookie pieces.

Assembly
1. Preheat oven to 350°F (180°C).
2. Pour filling into chilled Cookie Crumb Crust. Bake 1-1/2 hours. Turn off oven. Open door slightly and let cake cool in oven 1 hour. Remove from oven and cool cake completely on wire rack. Cover and refrigerate at least 6 hours. Remove springform and transfer cake to a serving platter.

Serves 12.

Brownie Points Pie

Tiger: *This is for the players I have known who could gain weight without gaining points—somehow they always managed to stay on the coach's good side.*

Kasey: *This rich, crustless pie is best with ice cream or whipped cream.*

2 cups	chocolate chips	500 mL
3 Tbsp.	butter	50 mL
3	eggs	3
1 cup	sugar	250 mL
1 Tbsp.	instant coffee	15 mL
1/2 tsp.	vanilla extract	2 mL
6 Tbsp.	flour	100 mL
1/4 tsp.	baking powder	1 mL
1/4 tsp.	salt	1 mL
1/2 cup	chocolate chips	125 mL
1/4 lb.	walnuts, chopped (**optional**)	125 g

1. Preheat oven to 350°F (180°C).
2. Melt chocolate chips and butter in a double boiler over warm (not hot) water, stirring just until mixture reaches a fudgelike texture.
3. In a mixing bowl, with an electric beater, beat eggs, sugar, coffee and vanilla until fluffy. Blend in flour, baking soda and salt. Mix in the melted chocolate chips. Add 1/2 cup chocolate chips and walnuts. Pour into a 10-inch (25-cm) pie pan.
4. Bake 35–40 minutes or until sides rise slightly. Cool thoroughly before slicing.

Serves 8–10.

Sudden Death by Chocolate

Tiger: *Like few things in heaven, this tastes the same in English and French (La mort au chocolat). I'm not much on imports but if you can get this, take it. Kasey feared it was "pretentious" but I think that word reminds me of imports anyway. Try Baker's—if you've got it, use it.*
Kasey: *A chocolate pâté with raspberry sauce, and it may be made in advance. A perfect ending.*

1 cup	butter, at room temperature	250 mL
2 cups	unsweetened cocoa	500 mL
6 oz.	imported bittersweet chocolate, broken into 1/2-inch (1-cm) pieces	170 g
1 cup	whipping cream	250 mL
8 large	egg yolks	8 large
3/4 cup	sugar	175 mL
1/4 cup	Scotch whiskey	50 mL

1. Line the long sides and bottom of a 1-qt. (1-L) narrow French porcelain terrine or an 8-1/2 × 4-1/2 inch (1.5-L) loaf pan with a sheet of parchment paper or wax paper extending 3 inches (7.5 cm) over each side. Spray the paper and insides of the container with an oil and set aside.
2. Place butter and cocoa in the bowl of a food processor and, using metal blade, process until very smooth, scraping sides of bowl as necessary. Set aside.
3. Place chocolate in a double boiler over warm (not hot) water and stir until just melted. Set aside to cool.
4. Whip cream and set aside.
5. Combine egg yolks and sugar in a large mixing bowl. With an electric beater, at medium speed, beat until thick and pale yellow (3–5 minutes).
6. Add melted chocolate to the egg mixture and beat until well blended. Add the butter-cocoa mixture and beat until smooth. Stir in Scotch whiskey and then gently fold in the whipped cream.
7. Transfer mixture to the prepared container and smooth the top evenly with a spatula. Gently tap the container on the counter to eliminate air bubbles. Cover and freeze overnight.
8. Before serving, remove chocolate pâté from the freezer and let sit at room temperature for 30 minutes. Run a thin knife along each short side of the container and lift pâté out by the paper wings. Invert on a rectangular platter and carefully peel off the parchment.

9. Splatter Raspberry Sauce from a distance onto a large dessert plate. With a knife dipped in hot water, slice pâté crosswise into 1/2-inch (1-cm) slices and place a slice on each plate. Serve remaining sauce on the side.

Serves 16.

Raspberry Sauce

2–15-oz. pkgs.	frozen raspberries in syrup	2–425-g pkgs.
1 Tbsp.	cornstarch	15 mL
1/4 cup	raspberry liqueur, Kirsch or brandy	50 mL

1. In a food processor or in two batches in an electric blender, blend thawed raspberries with their syrup at high speed until thoroughly pureed and slightly frothy. Place a strainer over a saucepan and strain berries to remove seeds.
2. In a small bowl, dissolve cornstarch in liqueur. Stir into raspberry puree.
3. Stir constantly over moderate heat until sauce comes to a boil and thickens.

Makes about 2 cups (500 mL).

Flaming Omelette

Tiger: *Anyone can make this but not everyone can eat it. Those with handlebar mustaches should stay away from the flames.*
Kasey: *This is an easy last-minute dessert you can always rely on to make an impression.*

2 Tbsp.	butter	25 mL
2 Tbsp.	brown sugar	25 mL
2	bananas, peeled	2
1 cup	sliced strawberries	200 mL
8	eggs	8
8 Tbsp.	water	100 mL
1 tsp.	sugar	5 mL
4 Tbsp.	butter	60 mL
8 Tbsp.	brandy	100 mL
2 cups	sour cream	500 mL
	whole strawberries for garnish	

1. In a skillet over medium heat, melt butter. Add brown sugar. Cut bananas in half lengthwise and then crosswise. Sauté bananas for 1 minute on each side. Cover, remove from heat and keep warm.
2. In a bowl, use a fork to beat eggs, water and sugar vigorously for 30 seconds.
3. In a well-seasoned 8-inch (20-cm) omelette pan or skillet over medium-high heat, melt 1 Tbsp. (15 mL) butter until it foams.
4. Pour 1/2 cup (125 mL) egg mixture into pan and allow to set for a few seconds. Tilt pan and slide rapidly back and forth on the burner, lifting edges of omelette with pancake turner to allow uncooked egg on top to flow under cooked portion. When top is moist and creamy, add 2 slices sautéed bananas and 1/4 cup (50 mL) sliced strawberries. Cook 30 seconds. Omelette should be slightly brown on the outside, creamy but not liquid on the inside.
5. With pancake turner, fold omelette in half. Add 2 Tbsp. (25 mL) brandy to pan and ignite. When flames subside, spoon 1/2 cup (125 mL) sour cream on top of omelette. Transfer from pan onto warmed serving plate and garnish with whole strawberries. Serve immediately. Repeat with remaining ingredients to make 3 more omelettes.

Makes 4 omelettes.

Centre Ice

Tiger: *I used to call this The Red Line, but the more I made it the more I thought Centre Ice suited it better. Send me a note if you don't agree.*
Kasey: *Try this with Brownie Points Pie (page 95).*

2 cups	water	500 mL
2-1/2 cups	sugar	625 mL
8 cups	fresh strawberries	2 L
1/4 cup	lemon juice	50 mL

1. In a saucepan, combine the water and sugar and bring to a boil. Simmer 5 minutes. Remove from heat. Pour the syrup into a bowl and chill in refrigerator.
2. Remove stems from strawberries. Place strawberries in the bowl of a food processor or electric blender and puree. Add the syrup and lemon juice to food processor or blender. Pour the mixture into the cannister of a hand-cranked or electric ice cream machine and freeze according to the manufacturer's instructions.

Makes 2 qts. (2L).

Index

Acknowledgements

We wish to thank those who contributed expertise and recipes, especially Rick Antonson for his enthusiastic involvement; Mae Livingstone and Sue Kelly for testing recipes; Judith Filtness for preparing the manuscript; Lori Ramsden for the metrication; cooking professionals Anne Milne, Bert Greene and Julie Watson, and hockey enthusiasts Glen Mennie and Jack Leonard.

The publisher would like to thank the following people and companies for their assistance: Alex Gair & Sons, Basic Stock, B.C. Fruit Wholesalers Co-operative Association, Fred "Cyclone" Taylor Sporting Goods, Import & Domestic Trading Co., Inform Interiors, Kelbert Trophies, The Market Kitchen, Midland Appliances Distributors, Money's Mushrooms, Otto Friedl Jewellers, Scandinavian Antiques, Ross Slack, Woodburn Stoves and Barbeques.

Food styling by Eileen Dwillies
Photo assistance by Michael Morissette and Jay Shaw
Propping assistance by Frank Vena and Judy Bates

p. 17: shirt—Ross Slack; large trophy and plaque—Kelbert Trophies; porcelain dishes—Basic Stock; produce—Money's Mushrooms and B.C. Fruit Wholesalers Co-operative Association

p. 18: stove top—Midland Appliances Distributors; omelette pan—Basic Stock; plate and cutlery (Mikasa)—Import & Domestic Trading Co.; stop watch—Otto Friedl Jewellers; produce—B.C. Fruit Wholesalers Co-operative Association

p. 35: stove top—Midland Appliances Distributors; referee shirt and whistle—Fred "Cyclone" Taylor Sporting Goods; saucepan, salad bowl, salt shaker, ramekin and pot holders—Basic Stock; platter and wine glass—Inform Interiors

p. 36: hibachi—Woodburn Stoves and Barbeques; shirt—Ross Slack; knife—The Market Kitchen; produce—Money's Mushrooms and B.C. Fruit Wholesalers Co-operative Association

p. 53: barbeque—Woodburn Stoves and Barbeques; shirt—Ross Slack; D'Arcy plate—The Market Kitchen; barbeque fork—Basic Stock; produce—Money's Mushrooms and B.C. Fruit Wholesalers Co-operative Association

p. 54 and front cover: table top—Alex Gair and Sons; shirt—Ross Slack; pilsner glass—Inform Interiors; knife—The Market Kitchen; produce—Money's Mushrooms and B.C. Fruit Wholesalers Co-operative Association

p. 71: shirt—Ross Slack; salad bowl and fork—Inform Interiors; puck—Fred "Cyclone" Taylor Sporting Goods; produce—B.C. Fruit Wholesalers Co-operative Association

p. 72: bowl and spoon—Scandinavian Antiques